Seeing Things

John Malone

Seeing Things

Acknowledgements

Some of these poems have appeared in
The School Magazine (NSW) and the *NZ School Journal*.
'On Being Compared to a Gnat' has appeared in
The Friendly Street Reader.

Many thanks to Graham Rowlands for editing this collection
and to Stephen Matthews for taking it on.

To Caty, with love and gratitude
for helping me stay buoyant during heavy times.

Seeing Things
ISBN 978 1 76041 100 8
Copyright © text John Malone 2016
Cover image © olly – Fotolia

First published 2016 by
GINNINDERRA PRESS
PO Box 3461 Port Adelaide 5015 Australia
www.ginninderrapress.com.au

Contents

Off With the Fairies	7
1948	8
In a Jiff	9
Seeing Things	10
Cows in a Paddock	11
Random Thoughts About Mirrors	12
Black Hole	13
About a Girl	14
Certificate	15
Getting it Right	16
Bike Boy	17
The Other Virtues	19
Affliction	20
Green Gazebo 1	21
Green Gazebo 2	22
The Two of Us	23
Stealth	24
That Pale Pink Stain	25
Tongues	26
I Didn't See It	27
I Love the Way	28
Beach Butterflies	29
Wagtails	30
Cenotaph	31
Party Animals	32
The First	33
A Pink Hippo	34
Your Meds	35
My Little Cloth Heart	36
Thief	37

People from Porlock	39
Inkwells	40
The Red Pencil Sharpener	41
I'm Good at Last Lines	42
A Poem Without Words	43
Not Just Another Snail Poem	44
Too Much	45
The Evidence	46
Lucky	47
Lost	48
Nestling Fallen on Hard Times	49
My Inner Fish	50
Ant	51
On Being Compared to a Gnat	52
The Diner	53
Zen Sandwich	54
Lepidoptera	55
Yield	56
Harpooning a Haiku	57

Off With the Fairies

Where's Uncle Midge? I asked one sunny afternoon.
He's off with the fairies again, Aunty said
Then quickly changed the topic. But I stayed on.
Off with the fairies? How did Aunty know?
Did he leave a note saying he'd be back
By so and so a time? It was hard to imagine
Uncle frolicking with the fairies if that is what
One does when one is 'off with them'.
He seemed too weighty and substantial for that.
And anyway where was he off to?
Where does one go when one is 'off with the fairies'?
I looked out the lounge room window out
To the backyard where uncle often used to wander
But there was nothing – only a pair
Of garden gnomes who seemed to be smiling
As if they had seen something.

1948

My father kept a copy by the side of his bed.
Occasionally I would sneak a look, pulled
by the lurid sketch on the cover: a scantily clad
blonde fighting off a man with a pistol.
I imagined how it would end. Once when no one
was home, I flipped through its well-thumbed
pages when I found the passage where the bullet
enters her soft white belly. I immediately grew
as stiff as that pistol.
                After Dad died I kept a copy
in a draw by my bed which I drew upon from
time to time.

In a Jiff

I'll be there in a jiff,
the nurse promises.
I tell Mum.
I can't wait much longer,
she says; how long
is a jiff?
I don't know, I say. How long
do you think?
We speculate.
A minute goes by.
Two. Three.
Already longer than the few tics
the nurse promised
last Sunday.
Mum pushes the caller button
again & again.
You're pushing it, I say. She'll
only be a jiff.
At that moment she bursts
through the door.
I check my watch.
A jiff, I note, is
five-and-three-quarter minutes long.

Seeing Things

At 6 a.m. the curtains part.
She sits up. Blinks.
Chimpanzee in the jacarandas
monkey around.
Two zulu warriors on the front lawn
play tom-toms.
A girl with a mousey face
squeaks hello from the corner
of the room.
She blinks again.
The black numerals on her clock face
detach themselves
scurry around like ants on speed.
The Sacred Heart of Jesus bleeds
onto the cabinet.
Visions visionaries would give
their eyeballs for.
You never know what you'll see
next
she says.
Is it the tablets?
The lollies she eats before she
settles down?
A hardening of the arteries
leading to the brain?
No one knows.
Still, each time we come to visit
our eyes are opened.

Cows in a Paddock

Someone told me once you can tell what the weather
will be like by studying cows in a paddock.
If the cows are standing, so she said, there'd be
a good chance of rain, whereas if they are prostrate
you could count on fine weather. Or it might have been
the other way around. What a load of bull, I thought.
What if half are standing and half are lying down?
Would that mean a 50% chance of fine weather, or to put it another way,
a 50% chance of rain, depending on whether you were
a glass half-full or a glass half-empty person? It seemed a little dodgy.
What if, for instance, in one paddock all the cows were prostrate
while in another, they were practising synchronised standing?
Wouldn't one cancel out the other? And why only cows?
What about prognosticating pigs, lambs, billy goats?
I decided to go back to the Bureau forecasts.
At least they get it right half the time.

Random Thoughts About Mirrors

mirrors never lie: sideshow mirrors only distorts the truth
you can look a mirror in the eye but it won't blink first
ceiling mirrors are up themselves
wall mirrors have hang-ups
mirrors continually surprise us in the act of being ourselves
mirrors both give and receive   simultaneously
during the day when everyone's at work do mirrors
   contemplate their navel
are one-way mirrors guilty of duplicity
do cracked mirrors have an image problem
mirrors are true philosophers: they are constantly reflecting
some mirrors have rear vision
what happens to mirrors in the dark

Black Hole

You're a black hole
a neutron star
sucking in
everything around you
down your vortex of spin.

There should be warning signs
warning lights
all around you:
Do Not Approach.
Stay Out Of View.

You're a cliff face.
A minotaur
in your labyrinth of need.
A morality tale
everyone should read.

You're a bad news story
that crops up
every other day.
One I'm tired of hearing.
Go away!

About a Girl

Her name is Mandy and she loves to laugh.
She's Sagittarius and I'm Capricorn,
the Centaur and the Goat.
I don't know how compatible they are
or whether all that laughter would get up my goat
and whether she wants a man
or a stand-up comedian.
Her profile pic is a little blurry which may be intentional.
She refers to her physique as 'voluptuous' & 'Rubensesque'
often synonyms for 'overweight'.
She has broad musical taste citing George Michael and
    Simply Red.
She hastens to add she is not a cook
and is not on earth to make men happy.
She is looking for a man with no emotional baggage.
She is planning a trip to Borneo
And I will NOT be going with her.

Certificate

I'm looking for my birth certificate
once again
to prove that I exist.
They seem to need convincing.
Isn't it obvious? I ask
but obviously it isn't.
They need that slip of paper.
In fact they insist upon it.
Doubting Thomases! I think
almost inviting them
to touch me.
But I hold back
almost afraid to touch myself.
What if…?
Perhaps I've gone around kidding myself
all these years.
Yes, I think, that slip of paper would help.
I hunt for it furiously.
If only to convince myself.

Getting it Right

It really was a bad line.
Do you know where I can get
some change, she asked –
a little teenage, a little dowdy
then added, for a sandwich
or something?
I pointed to the jeweller's
the travel agency across the road
adding, they've got plenty of money
they should be able to help.
Fuck you, she mumbled
as it hit me
as she hit on
someone else.
I almost called her back.

Bike Boy

An orange flare
of hair
      a kilt
arms, legs, chest bare
      tattooed
like a snake
that BMX he rides
like a skate-
board
feet on the saddle
the dazzle

& crow
of his act
as he works the crowd
like a stand-up
heckling passers-by
twirling

fiery clubs
like Catherine wheels
daggers, carving knives
the threat of severed limbs
& that body
taut, slim

& cocky
as he rips out the chainsaw
its raunchy buzz driving
the crowd back
               back
                    back
as he hurls it
again & again   into the air
saying 'if you like it shout yair'

& the flair
as he holds out his cap
'you don't have to pay but
guilt's a heavy burden'

then turns on that posh woman
'don't walk away, madam, it only
makes you look cheap'

The Other Virtues

At assemblies, speech nights, seminars
they're urged to
try harder
reach higher
are pumped up by
former Olympians
netball champions
the youngest ever
young achiever
of the year
but where are the others:
the layabouts, dreamers, wastrels –
those who've climbed down
the ladder of success
and made a fist of it
or never bothered
to climb at all
failures who couldn't fail
to entertain
exemplars of the other virtues:
apathy, indolence, contentment?
Students need choice

Affliction

The word 'Elizabeth' got me.
When people asked where I worked
I had to say it
syllable by syllable
but not so slowly people
thought me dumb.
A breath beforehand helped.
Other words obtruded
words that caught me up
that I couldn't get into
like a claustrophobe
before a lift.
I learned to word switch
to an easier word
one that rolled off
the tongue.
Though I still trembled
before an audience
like the king* who was
subject to stuttering.
But then I remembered
there were others –
Lewis Carroll
Isaac Newton
even Aesop
whose thoughts often outran
the tired tortoise of his tongue.

*King George VI

Green Gazebo 1

I have no faith, I have no credo
When I sit beneath the green gazebo.
Everything is as it is.
Life retains its whirr and whiz,
Its pulse and libido.

Green Gazebo 2

I like to wear my tuxedo
When I dine beneath the green gazebo.
I raise a glass to one and all
To my daughters, my son Paul
and my ever present ego.

The Two of Us

'I work alone
and so do you

but every now and then
we become two.

I'm on the bottom,
you're on the top.

I am the comma,
you the full stop'

Stealth

I scared you last night.
I scared myself
When I turned on you suddenly.
The dishes on the shelf

Rattled, the ginger cat
Slunk away.
It didn't stop to hear
What I had to say.

But you had to listen.
There was chance for little else.
I scared you last night.
I scared myself.

That Pale Pink Stain

That pale pink stain won't go
That pale pink stain won't budge
From the Chinese Willow Pattern bowl
No matter how hard I scrub.

That pale pink stain's annoying.
That pale pink stain won't do.
It's a nasty discolouration
In an otherwise perfect blue.

What are you doing, my partner laughs
And her amusement grows.
You're not trying to remove
That perfect pale pink rose?!

It's part of the pattern, you goose
A lovely shade of pink.
Please put the bowl down right now
& leave it on the sink.

Tongues

Cat got your tongue?
my mother would say

and even now I sometimes
lose my tongue or become

tongue-tied; some people,
touched by the spirit,

speak in tongues; others,
by a darker spirit, speak

with forked tongues; still
others, tongue-in-cheek

though up close tongues
can never lie: *if you want*

to know if he loves you so
*it's in his kis*s

I Didn't See It

I didn't see it.
I wasn't watching.
I took my eye off the ball.
It may not have made a difference.
None at all.

It may have happened offstage.
In the wings.
Out of view.
But it happened just here.
Before me and you.

Was I complicit?
Were we?
Taking our eyes off the ball?
It may not have made a difference.
None at all.

I Love the Way

I love the way waves rise up from their seats like people at a concert standing to applause.
I love the way jetties wade out in the water without getting their knees wet.
I love how they stand so stout and sturdy without ever getting tired – or bored from standing in the one place
I love how baby cockles squiggle in the sand like kids when they first doodle.
I love the way the sea and sky hug at the horizon
how gulls fly in their loose little Vs in the space between like cars on their way from work
and finally I love how the sun sits like a bright burnished plate on the mantelpiece of the sea.

Beach Butterflies

The sky is full of butterflies
beach butterflies
rising and falling
in the strong sea breeze,
wings curved and colourful
as real butterflies:
brumby butterflies
tethered to earth-men
on surfboards below
skimming across the waves
holding on fiercely
as these butterflies buck and lunge
for freedom.

Wagtails

but for their size
they're the Rottweilers
of the bird world
these off-the-leash
off-their-tree
wannabe magpies
these black-white
concoctions of spite
feathered Furies
these snip-beaked
black-faced
in-your-face
chitterers
xenophobes of suburbia.
Anyone
in their yard
is a foreigner.

Cenotaph

With the sun dozing overhead
wreaths still green on the steps
the skateboarders come
clattering

scattering
tranquillity like a scurry of gulls.
Up and down the steps they leap
and crash
daggy acrobats in baggy shorts
and baseball caps

turned backwards
outraging shoppers and shop assistants
the diggers who've come
to reflect.

Above them
the marbled Angel of Death
looks coldly on.

Party Animals

like a party out of control, you
can hear them streets away

ghost galahs guffawing in the gums
drunk with plenty, wheeling

and cavorting, screeching across
the oval like hoons in

souped-up holdens; but later as
shadows lengthen, they

settle, little white flags of surrender,
to the equanimity of evening

The First

Someone has to be the first.
Someone has to walk through the door
sit down at the table
before the others.
Someone has to take the first bite
of the cherry
be the early bird if worms
are to be taken.
Someone has to drop the stone in the pool
to set the ripples going
to throw the first stone for the stoning
to begin.
Someone has to be the first cab off the rank.
Someone has to set the ball rolling if anything
is to happen.

A Pink Hippo

You open your mouth. A pink hippo comes out. You scratch your ear, a purple gorilla. You blow your nose, a polka-dot egret. You pass wind, an emerald marmoset. You wonder what will come next. You go to the toilet. You piss piranhas. Defecate falcons. Can I have some more you ask the anaesthetist but the anaesthetist has gone, the effects wearing off just as an oleaginous eel slithers from the long wound in your leg from which the surgeon removed veins for your blocked arteries.

Your Meds

'Have you had
your meds?'
'Yes, I have,'
I said.
'One for my chest,
one for my arms
and one to keep me
steady & calm.'
'And did you use
your bowels? Did you…?'
'Yes,' I said.
'Wee and poo.'
'Thank you,'
he said,
nodding his head.
'That will do.'

My Little Cloth Heart

I've had it for a fortnight.
I use it on and off.
I clutch it to my real heart
when I splutter, or cough.

It helps absorb vibrations
shocks that might cause harm.
It keeps my body steady
and my spirit calm.

It is soft and cuddly
off-white and bare.
Like Linus and his blanket
I take it everywhere.

Thief

I am a thief.
Watch me.
I am never at rest.
My tools
are my ears, my eyes
my prey
the streets of my city.
I scan
for the constrained face
the frown
or smile that betrays.
I listen into
conversations.
Priestlike
I elicit confessions.
I watch for
the unguarded sentence,
the revealing phrase.
I am the one
with the notebook
opposite you
in the bus.
I am the one
with the slightly intent look
at your side.
Watch out for me.
I am the purloiner
of language.

I snatch words
and use them
as my own.
For I am a thief
a thief of words.

People from Porlock

After boarding the bus, I pulled out my notebook and began to write the poem pounding in my head.

But then I looked up and saw my aunt sitting next to me.

'What are you writing?' she asked.

'A poem,' I said. 'Just a poem.' And then I put it down.

What could I do? She was my aunt.

We got to talking till her stop came up.

When she got off, I had my chance, lowering my pen to finish the first line. I felt I was on a roll.

But then the bus was turned into a sardine can.

A young bloke sat next to me, his iPod blaring.

It was The White Stripes live from Livid and they were 'looking for a home'.

How could I not listen? It was Meg and Jack.

Just as well he got off when he did.

I took up my pen once more.

But then a cross-eyed man slumped beside me, his hair a rat's tail, his skin studded with tats.

How could I not look, his arms a graphic novel?

Then there was the woman who took his place, shouting abuse into her mobile.

I winced at every punch.

The guy on the other end was out for the count then he got up and then she started again. Wham! Bam! You could taste the blood.

Luckily Coleridge didn't board this bus while he was thinking 'Kubla Khan'.

He wouldn't have written a thing!

Inkwells

When I was a kid we had inkwells at school,
one to a desk, topped up with ink the colour
of the deep sea. I'd dip a pen in the well
and write about the sea: how ships seem to sail
along the curve of its edge, how it breathes
in and out like all living things, and how birds
fly over it, gazing down through the portholes
of their eyes.
                When I finished writing, I'd look
  at all the runny blue letters curved and flowing
  like waves, and I'd be down at the beach.
                One day it all came to an end.
Inkwells went out. Ballpoints came in.

The Red Pencil Sharpener

I am looking down the barrels of
the red pencil sharpener
its holes
big as drainpipes
fat as full moons
flared like the nostrils
of horses;
they are
deep wells
dark tunnels
O-shaped mouths hungry
for pencils

The red pencil sharpener sharpens
my imagination

I'm Good at Last Lines

I'm good at last lines.
I really am.
The rest of my poems are crap but the last lines are really something.
I'm thinking of bringing out a book of poems with only their last lines.
It's a little unorthodox, I know.
And the trouble is the last lines would by default end up being the first.
Even if I put the last line at the bottom of the page with a blank space above, it'd still be the first line.
I don't know a way around this.
Perhaps if I wrote a great poem and didn't worry about the last line it just might work.
The trouble is, no matter how great the poem, it'd have to have a last line.
I could still write, I suppose, a great last line to a great poem but it's a big ask. It really is.
I'm losing confidence.
Now I can't even write a great last line to this poem.

A Poem Without Words

I'm writing a poem without words.
It goes for 4.52
a little longer if you build in
the pauses.
There's one point where I get
really worked up.
Words just can't express it.
Still, people will say,
it's a bit long isn't it?
but what can I do?
There's just so much
I don't want to say.
I'm thinking of bringing a book out
of wordless poems
in various styles. of course.
It should leave people speechless.

Not Just Another Snail Poem

I am writing a poem about a snail.
It is coming along rather slowly.
I check out if there are other poems
about snails. There are.
Elizabeth Bishop imagined she was one.
Thom Gunn wrote about their 'pale antlers'.
Richard Lovelace wrote about the 'compendious' shape-
   shifting snail and took over 60 lines to do it.
Mine's not so ambitious.
But I liked Matisse's snail best.
It's a collage which looks nothing like a snail.
Perhaps that's the answer.
I try writing a poem about a snail in which I say nothing
about a snail.
It is suitably loopy.
Bit by bit I tease it from the hard shell of my brain.

Too Much

It's a good day, I said, the sun angling through the red gums hooking our attention.

I don't know, he said, Friday was pretty impressive too (referring to the hailstorm)

then he looked at me, knowing I'm a poet, and said, you gunna write about it?

& I said, without thinking, when I get time, Mark, when I get time

& I thought about it afterwards, how you could write about almost anything at all

even the least bit startling – a rock maybe metamorphosing into a frog, the hurtle of creek water rounding a bend, a screech of cockatoos tearing up the sky

there'd be so many you wouldn't know where to stop. You'd be writing all day

& the night would hold some surprises too – a spider abseiling down a branch, the colouration of a sunset or moonscape, the soft sounds of love –

everything offering itself into words: there'd be no end to it; in the end you'd have to

avert your eyes, close your mind, do what you were told never to do and NOT listen

to the Muse; only then would you get some peace, the world so ablaze with glory

the problem is not too little but too much.

The Evidence

I buried it, of course.
What would you have done?
The earth forgives.
And forgets.
Others might not understand.
Might draw the wrong conclusions.
Or worse – the right ones.
There were questions of course.
By the neighbours.
The authorities.
But I played dumb.
Said nothing.
Mute as the earth.
They sniffed something, I know
those with sharp noses.
But what could they prove?
The only worry was the dog
pawing, pawing at the ground.

Lucky

Penny has a new pet.
A Labrador called Lucky.
It's what she always wanted.
Well, almost.
He sits, jumps and spins around
and chases after frisbees.
Penny takes him for long walks
on the screen.
When he's tired, Penny puts him
to bed.
His kennel is a black microchip.
When Penny slips it in the game console
each morning,
Lucky comes out to play.
He woofs with delight and rubs
his snowy head against the screen.
Penny would love to cuddle him.

Lost

I met him on a winding path leading
to the zoo. I had lost my girl. He had lost
the plot though I did not know it then.
We talked briefly. Before his accomplishments
– his CV baggy with published poems – I
was lost for words. 'Take care,' I remember
him saying. 'He's always had his head
in the clouds,' a fellow poet once said.
Perhaps that's why he climbed to the roof
of a big city hotel and stepped off.

Nestling Fallen on Hard Times

All week the ants have been at it
picking at the flesh and feathers
revealing the lean elegant lines
within
the fretted ribs
the railway track of spine
that noble head
much in the same way
as sculptors are said
to reveal
chip by chip
the form already there
inside the marble

My Inner Fish

'See those starting blocks over there?
Those three blue concrete stumps?
That's where I learned to swim.
There was a pool there once –
a saltwater one and a coach who
one chilly morning threw me in.
"Nothing else seems to work," he said.
"You choose. Sink or swim."
That's where I found my inner fish.
Waterlogged, I struggled to the side.
But I was fine. Unlike my lost uncle
"Adelaide's finest swimmer," Dad said.
"Dead at twenty-five. The river took him."
Dad always spoke of Uncle Lorry.
That's why I learned to swim.'

Ant

There's an ant in the kitchen levitating just above the bread board.

A black, squiggly thing, he hangs there like a thought balloon, too small perhaps for the pull of gravity.

A few other ants go about their business below as if it is an old party trick they had seen many times before.

But I hadn't.

I feel like applauding.

Instead I stand back and watch from behind the pantry door so he won't get self conscious and fall.

Occasionally he glances up and perhaps spotting me does a little walk like the astronauts do in space. But mostly he just hangs there.

I keep waiting for an encore.

But that apparently is it.

After a while I get bored. I close the door and leave him to it.

On Being Compared to a Gnat

You have the attention span,
he said,
of a gnat.

I thought (briefly)
about that:

the skim
the look;
the review
not the book;

the single
not the CD;
a movement not
the whole symphony;

the single poem –
a story won't do –
especially if short
think haiku.

Life's short.
Try this, that.
Stay light,
says the gnat.

The Diner

he sits there alone
hermetically sealed in his
self assurance

the discomfiture
of silent couples looking
across at him

head rimmed with hair
like the tonsure of a monk; he is
calm, meditative

around him the graffiti
of small talk; no magazines, newspaper,
mobile phone

no clutter – a white
tablecloth, a glass of water, an
oversized white plate

the spatchcock and buck-
wheat assembled on it thoughtfully
as a haiku

Zen Sandwich

I am eating my zen sandwich by the side
   of a blue lake. I hear the sound of
      two wings flapping.

A fawn falcon plunges down the side
   of the volcanic cone, its claws extended
      like the landing gear of a plane.

As it skims across the surface – a sail-winged
   skater – the talons lacerate the taut
      blue skin of that lake. It bleeds blue.

Lepidoptera

1. Mark

that scab: a
rust-red butterfly resting
on my brow

2. Thinking

my mind flits from thought
to waste thought: more tawdry moth
than bright butterfly

3. Summer in the City

scents of beauty:
behind these sunnies my eyes are
sly butterflies flitting
from one girl
to
another

4. *Glioblastoma Multi-forme*

unfurling into
both hemispheres of the brain
like the wings

of a butterfly:
the tumour; or more accurate
yet

the rabid
dragon-like pterosaur,
Dsungaripterus

Yield

a bright rainbow
scythes
the air:
a gentle crop
of rain

Harpooning a Haiku

the haiku lunges
out of the dark ocean of text
its flanks bejewelled

by sun, the way
a whale lunges out of the water
in Oban Bay

www.ingramcontent.com/pod-product-compliance
Lightning Source LLC
Chambersburg PA
CBHW062203100526
44589CB00014B/1933